This book belongs to:

Dedication

This book is dedicated to all beings very big and all beings very small.

Harmony

Visionary and Author - Suzanne Sullivan

Co-Author and Editor - Pamela Breeze Bahr

Illustrator - Wendy Lorenzana

Chip the Monk Foundation is a non-profit public charity operated exclusively for educational and charitable purposes within the meaning of Section 501(c)(3) of the Internal Revenue Code of 1986.

Tax deductible donations are gratefully accepted to support this important work.
Please visit our website to make a donation.

Chipthemonk.com
Facebook: Chipthemonk

CHIP THE MONK

Be kind to your mind

PART I

THE GREAT FORGETTING

A long time ago harmony was felt by all,
all beings very big and all beings very small.
Everyone danced and sang happy songs.
They laughed and played the whole day long.

Then one day something happened
that was stranger than strange,
and quick as a wink,
everything changed.

People forgot how to have fun and be glad.
They spent their days feeling upset and mad.
Something terrible and dark had invaded their lives,
causing chaos and troubles to rumble and rise.

The invader was Pea Brain, a mean little pea,
who didn't want laughter or harmony.
The meanie green pea blew unhappy bubbles,
changing bright-sparkly thoughts into boo-hooey troubles.

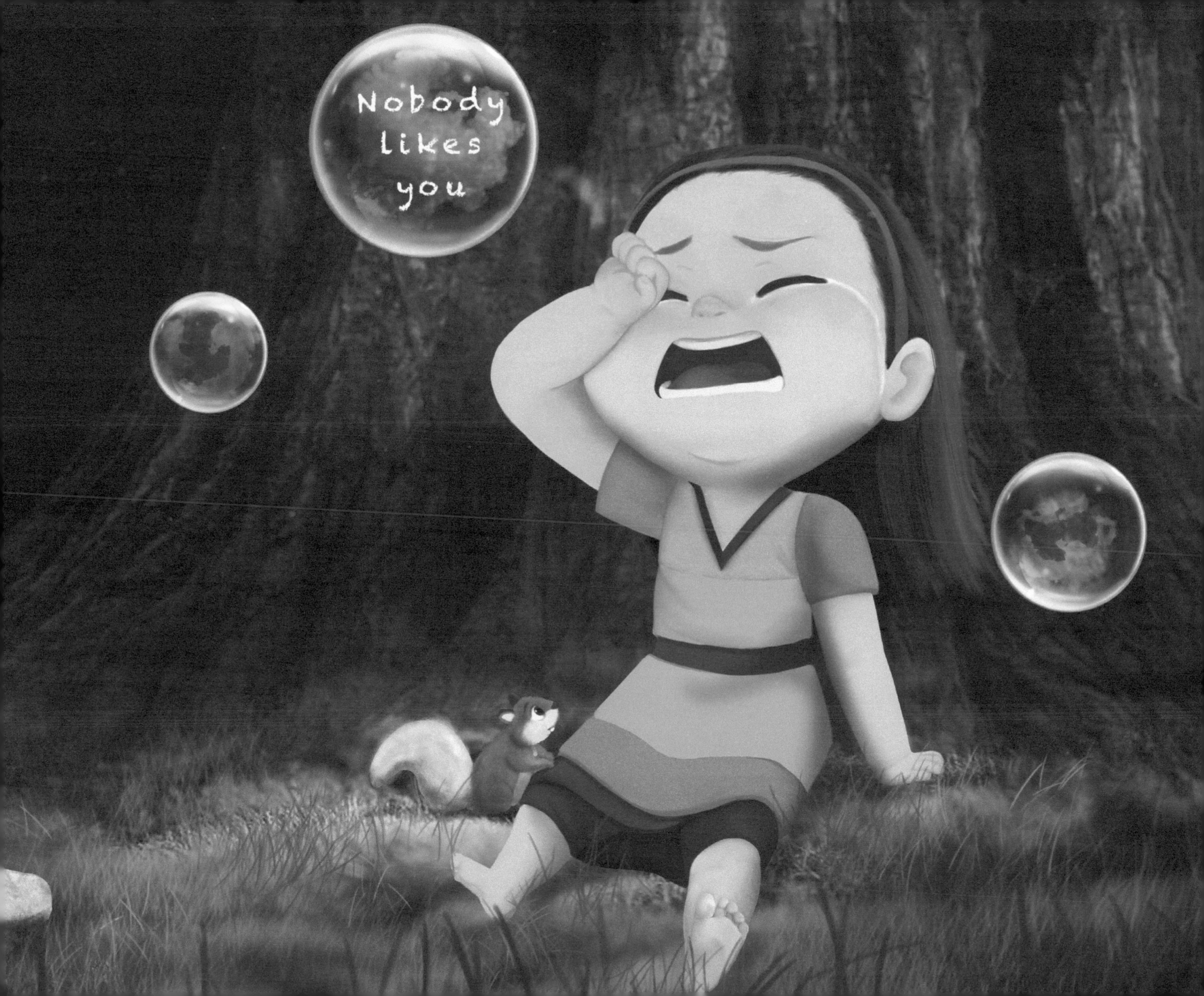
Nobody likes you

Pea Brain appeared from out of nowhere,
making people feel bad for he just didn't care!
They all believed what the trouble bubbles said
and let the ugly thoughts go straight to their head.

After a while there were no more smiles,
only hopeless faces for miles and miles.
The world fell into an ocean of sorrow,
without any hope for a better tomorrow.

The Harmony Animals knew what was true,
and sensed right away what it was they should do.
They journeyed to a place that had once been their home
to ask for help and a path to be shown.

There was Dolly the Llama, who helps dissolve drama,
the Harmony Bees, who are always at ease,
Timidy the Turtle, who helps overcome hurdles,
and Holy the Cow, who lives in the WOW!

Harmony Village was the place of their birth.
They returned there to WiseOne, who came from the earth.
They knew that her wisdom would help them get clear
on how to help people let go of their fear.

Beneath the shade of the Wisdom Tree,
they waited for WiseOne patiently.
They sat as quietly as they could,
and her face began to appear in the wood.

She listened as they told the very sad tale,
but she already knew it was just a bad spell.
WiseOne had seen that this might come to be
if people were tricked by the lies of the pea.

Pea Brain, she explained, isn't actually real
and has no power over how people feel.
But when they believe the meanie green pea,
this is what they will start to see.

WiseOne told them that a guide would soon come
to show how the spell could be over and done.
They would work as a team, brave and wise,
to put an end to the pea's dreadful lies.

After listening to WiseOne they felt so blessed
and settled in for a much-needed rest.
They peacefully waited for the guide to come
to bring back the joy and the bright-sparkly fun.

PART II

THE ARRIVAL

WiseOne knew that the time was near
for the guide she foresaw to finally appear.
One day she felt a small little twitch
and thought it might be something to itch.

But when she turned her head, what did she see?
A baby chipmunk asleep on a branch of her tree.
When he slowly opened his bright-twinkly eyes,
WiseOne knew right away he had finally arrived.

Holding the little one close to her heart,
she went to the village with great news to impart.
The animals marveled as they gathered around
and gazed at the treasure that WiseOne had found.

They were thrilled to meet Chip, their new little friend,
who would help bring the gloom in the world to an end.
They jumped and they jiggled, they sang and they wiggled!
They were so overjoyed that they fell down and giggled.

Chip grew up, loved and free,
with WiseOne and friends near the Wisdom Tree.
But there came a day when he had to be shown
what was happening outside of his safe, happy home.

WiseOne had known from the very start
that Chip had to know this terrible part.
They sat together so he could see
all the chaos and upset unleashed by the pea.

When Chip saw Pea Brain for the very first time,
he felt scared that the pea was so mean and unkind.
Looking at WiseOne, his trembling voice small,
he asked her what would become of them all.

That's when she told him that he was the one.

She explained his mission and what was to come.

When Chip heard her words, he thought he'd heard wrong.

He was frightened for he felt that he wasn't that strong.

PART III

THE DECISION

You're
too
small

It's
scary

He ran back to the village and hid under his bed,

trying hard to forget what WiseOne had said.

For how could a sweet, gentle soul such as he

stand up to someone as mean as the pea?

You're not strong enough

Chip couldn't stop all the voices in his head
that were saying, "Don't do it—there's danger ahead!"
The thought of it all just filled him with dread.
"Perhaps," he thought, "I'll just stay here instead."

As Chip, all alone, tried hard to decide,
the animals stood patiently right outside.
Their powerful love slipped under his door,
surrounding him while he cried on the floor.

As he allowed its message to enter his mind,
he began to feel lighter and stronger inside.
And after three days, something started to change.
The voices got quiet, no trembling remained.

He bravely emerged from under his bed,
willing to accept what WiseOne had said.
He went out and found her under the tree
and said, "I trust what you see in me."

"I'm still a bit scared and small in size,
but I feel I can see through Pea Brain's lies."
She assured him once more that he was the one
and that his training would help all his fear be undone.

A celebration began once the news got around
that Chip had said yes, that his strength had been found.
The animals promised to keep playing their parts,
surrounding Chip with all the love in their hearts.

PART IV

THE APPRENTICESHIP

Be afraid

You're stupid

Cry baby

Lazy

Good for nothing

Shame on you

Ugly

You're pathetic

Chip began his power-monk training,
which he did without any fuss or complaining.
WiseOne taught him a powerful rhyme
to say when a lie tried to enter his mind.

Grouchy

All you have to do
is remember it's not true.
Leave it, just leave it.
Simplydimply don't believe it!
Drop it, just drop it.
Remember you can pop it!

WiseOne showed him many wondrous and powerful ways
to remember the truth on the darkest of days.
Chip learned to stay calm and peaceful and centered
even when Pea Brain and his trouble bubbles entered.

He realized his work was to teach everyone
that inside the mind is where fear is undone.
Chip knew if people turned away from the pea,
they would remember how to be happy and free.

He pictured their joy and delighted surprise
as the pea dissolved right in front of their eyes.
Chip knew if the lies weren't believed anymore,
Pea Brain would be a pea puddle—lying on the floor!

Once Chip saw the truth, he had all that he needed.

His power-monk training was finally completed.

Clear in his mind and sure in his heart,

Chip knew that the time had come to depart.

Before Chip gathered his friends to go,
WiseOne had two gifts to bestow.
A simple monk's robe and a Harmony Token
to remind him that True Love can never be broken.

Chip and his friends walked down to the gate,
straight towards a world filled with lots of mistakes.
Looking back at WiseOne with love in his eyes,
Chip raised his paws in a heart-shaped goodbye.

He knew they could never be truly apart.
They were joined forever, heart to heart.

To Be Continued in Book Two...

AN INVITATION FROM CHIP THE MONK
AND THE HARMONY ANIMALS

In the collection of books to follow, we invite you to journey with us as we show people how to turn trouble bubbles into love bubbles.

You can begin your own power-monk training by answering the questions in Chip Chat as honestly as you can. There are no wrong answers!

Please accept our invitation to join us on this important mission.

We can't wait to see you on the road!

Love,
Chip and the Harmony Animals

CHIP CHAT

 Do you have any trouble bubbles that are upsetting you?

 What do you do when you are feeling afraid?

 Is there someone you feel scared of who is mean and unkind?

 Who surrounds you with love when you are afraid?

 Have you ever felt scared like me?

 What did you learn from this story that will help you?

To connect with Chip, become his friend on 🅕

Gladitude is the Attitude!

For over twenty years, inspired ideas and creative friends have helped me to bring this book and its insightful message to fruition. From the moment Chip the Monk was conceived, it was clear that something very unique would be born.

Chip the Monk is a heartfelt collaboration, and I extend my immense gladitude to the many beautiful beings who helped bring this book into the world. It is a simple yet powerful reminder to us all that harmony and happiness come from within… no matter what trouble bubbles may appear!

Blessings,
Suzanne Sullivan

Visionary and Author - Suzanne Sullivan
Co-Author and Editor - Pamela Breeze Bahr
Illustrator - Wendy Lorenzana

Special thanks to Rita Chance, Uroš Slemenik, Laverne Sheppard, Arlene Samen, and Jackie Simpson

Printed in the USA
CPSIA information can be obtained
at www.ICGtesting.com
LVHW060906291023

762114LV00016B/68